# Mindset Secrets for Homes Sellers

WRITTEN BY BETH REBENSTORF

Copyright 2020, Beth Rebenstorf, All Rights Reserved

Published in the United States of America

ISBN-13: 9781659551549

No parts of this publication may be reproduced without correct attribution to the author of this book.

# Dedication

To Home Sellers of All Mindsets
Motivated or Curious
Certain or Tentative
Veteran or Novice

# Table of Contents

Introduction..................................................................05
Mindsets of Successful Sellers................................07
The Home Selling Journey........................................13
The Preparation Process..........................................14
Room by Room Review.............................................16
The Marketing Process ............................................23
The Emotional Magic of Soft Staging....................23
It's Show Time, Lights, Lights,
and More Lights.........................................................30
Pictures and Videos are Key ...................................32
Lifestyle and Views = Money Shots ......................33
Making Your Home a Box Office Hit......................45
Pin Point Price, How Important Is It Really? .......47
Types of Markets and What Means.......................40
Market Value, the Start Point for
All Decisions...............................................................42
Appraisal and How They Can Affect Sellers .......44
Pricing Strategies......................................................47
Multiple Offers ...........................................................49
Things That Do Matter to Market Value................51
Things That Do NOT Matter to Market Value .....52
The 10/10 Rule of Showings....................................53
Top 10 Seller Mistakes ..............................................55
What About iBuyers? Instant Online Offers?.......56
Types of Buyers/Financing and
Why That's Important ..............................................61
Conclusion...................................................................64

# Introduction

## Home Seller Secrets

Shifting mentally and emotionally from homeowner mindset to home seller mindset is an often overlooked but important indicator to how your home selling journey will unfold. Even the most experienced of travelers prepare for journeys by learning about local customs, language, money exchange, travel options, weather, fueling stations, safety precautions, and local guides. Even if they've been before, they update their knowledge, look at maps, and consider recent conditions. They prepare. Why? Because preparation minimizes the unknown which in turn reduces stress improves the desired outcome.

When you first begin the transition of thinking like a successful home seller, the magnitude of what you're about to undertake begins to take shape. When my husband and I, along with 10 other adventurers set our sights on a two-week motorcycle trip through the European Alps (yes we were younger then) booking a flight was simple. Planning the details of the two-week journey was anything but. Any one of decision by itself was simple. Having each decision work together with other decisions and requirements took focus, detailed knowledge, and coordinated preparation. The same is true for the real estate journey. Putting a sign in the yard and on the MLS is the easy part. Those are but 2 steps in thousands. It's all the hundreds of complexities most people don't know or assume won't happen that cause chaos, aggravation or failure.

For most families their home is their single largest asset. Few people are aware that one of every five homes that receives an offer, never actually closes. Meaning an offer is just the beginning of hundreds of steps that must occur before closing day and receiving your proceeds! Just like arriving at your destination for a trip is only the beginning -- the success of the trip depends on the many experiences that happen along the way.

## So what makes the difference? What do successful homes sellers do to avoid being the one of five that fails?

As a former teacher, entrepreneur and fortune 500 corporate executive, I began to recognize the importance of each person's mindset as it relates to a task, project, or role. As a teacher I learned that helping students adjust their mindset significantly improved their learning, comprehension, and decision making abilities. Some approaches were unsuccessful not because of the strategy, but because the student's mindset was not conducive to that strategy being effective. I recognized the same principle in the corporate world. Success, effectiveness, and results are very much affected by current mindset. I say current because mindsets change as we grow and evolve.

**Mindsets affect how we filter information, how we receive what is communicated, how we process and analyze -- ultimately how we make decisions. Basically our mindsets influence our decisions.**

They say it takes 10,000 hours to master a craft. As a trusted real estate advisor (since 2005) after distilling tens of thousands of hours and thousands of real life situations, I've observed the impact that different mindsets create. I've experienced the benefit of how adjusting mindset improves the process and results. Each decision at hundreds of decision points during the home selling journey determines are influenced by mindsets.

So in addition to sharing proven strategies and real-life examples, my gift is the focus on mindsets as you prepare, reflect, and ultimately make decisions during your home selling journey. For the purpose of this book I've narrow it down to 3 common mindsets that successful sellers share.

# Mindsets of Successful Sellers

## Mindset #1: Ask Good Questions and Seek Meaningful Interpretation

This is the part of each us, I call Wise Watson– the open-minded, unbiased, receptive seeker that searches for knowledge and insight that leads to good decisions. Wise Watson asks good questions and listens carefully, always looking to gain deeper, better awareness.

**Sellers that connect with their Wise Watson:**

- Gather information to accurately assess market conditions, buyer behaviors, best practices, and effective strategies. Consider insight and context for strategies that will best serve them.

- Seek out the best source for timely and accurate information to provide not just information, but meaningful interpretation of data and information.

- Listen openly to avoid looking for ways to support preconceived notions.

- Base decisions on the most current and accurate assumptions because they are aware flawed results are a result of flawed assumptions and what is not know can be very harmful.

Example: Because they understand that buyers have access to the information and data that appraisers and lenders use to determine fair market value (and the amount a lender will approve for a buyer's loan) sellers with an accurate understanding of current market conditions and market value avoid the temptation to price too high. But what is too high? If market value is $300K, what asking price becomes harmful to a seller? Is it $305K? $315K? $330K? $350K? By understanding both current market value (which changes) AND current buyer behaviors (that also change) they understand what will help them and what will harm them. They arm themselves with the right understanding to make their decisions – based on today's market continues and best practices.

A client of ours who runs a very successful business and has sold several properties was ready to sell a property. Even though he had sold numerous times, he always started his process by updating and confirming his understanding. His Wise Watson wanted a current and accurate assessment, a bit of a refresher on the process, and perspective on what would mean for his situation. Some of the insightful questions he asked:

- Are the 4 homes that sold in the last 90 days in my neighborhood good (acceptable) comparable properties to mine?

- What are the things appraisers consider when they do a valuation. How much can they vary?

- What have you experienced with the last 12-15 closings as it relates to appraisal values and contract prices.

- Remind me of the scale used for condition and quality ratings (referring to the C1-C6 and Q1-Q6 ratings in an appraisal.) How important is that and what does it mean for market price?

- How many homes failed to sell … (cancelled, expired, off market, back on market etc…)

His Wise Watson made sure the right questions were asked and understood. He had the information and interpretation of information to choose wisely.

## Mindset #2: Willingly Accept What Cannot Be Changed and Change What Can

We all struggle at some point to accept what is. When things don't go our way, or the market tells us something we don't particularly want to hear, its tempting to dig in, ignore, or point fingers. The sooner we reflect and focus on what we can change, the sooner we move towards the thing we really want. The "Accept or Change" Mindset—The Wise Watson within us that knows when we need to shift because the current attitude is not serving us well. Sellers that tap into that Wise Watcson adjust their mindset when they become aware of things that are simply not in their control.

They are honest with themselves about things they can change and can't change. They don't squander their time and energy on things they can't change but invest their time and attention on those things that will support their goal.

You've heard the adage "failing to prepare, is preparing to fail". Successful sellers view careful preparation as the path to the most reliable results.

> *"If you don't like something Change it.*
> *If you Can't Change it, Change your attitude."*
>
> — Maya Angelou

Example: While the age of a home can't be changed, the perception of how well maintained it is can. There are cost effective changes that make one property more appealing to current buyer preferences than another property. Likewise, a seller with a home that backs up to a busy street may have no objection to traffic noise in the back yard. However, the seller with a healthy "Accept or Change" mindset will accept that a considerable portion of buyers will not share that opinion.

They can't change the buyer's opinion, but they can prepare and price with that obstacle in mind.

The seller that taps in to their "Accept or Change" mindset will quickly make the adjustment needed to attract their buyer. Sellers that resist and object to buyers having an opinion different than theirs, are less likely to make the appropriate adjustment that will ultimately lead to the sale of their home.

This "Accept or Change" mindset can often be the difference between homes that sell and those don't.

> *"Who exactly seeks out a coach? Winners."*
> — Chicago Tribune

### Mindset #3: Seek Expert Guidance and Coaching

Successful sellers have a deep respect for the thousand of hours and dollars invested to master any craft. When they excel at what they do, in their area of expertise, they recognize the deep work required to become a master. They seek out a guide and coach they trust to lead, guide and protect during the selling journey.

### Who is Renee Grant?

Its unlikely you know of Renee Grant, but you will recognize her clients like: Carrie Underwood, Christina Aguilera, Tim McGraw, Faith Hill, Jason Aldean, Keith Urban, Huey Lewis, the Dixie Chicks, Miley Cyrus, Garth Brooks, Linda Ronstadt, Kenny Chesney, Martina McBride… to name a few! Renee is voice coach to all these artists. Its significant that the best of the best in all fields, have the mindset that its wise to seek guidance from a trusted coach.

It is very common to watch a football game and see the quarterback take a time out to consult with their coach. Athletes, CEO's Car Racers, Musicians, Actors, even Rodeo— the very best seek perspective and guidance to make the best

> *A good coach makes a huge difference, because they have a perspective and wisdom that only up-to-date current knowledge, real life experience, and the thousands of dedicated hours needed to have a high level of experience.*

possible decision. What are you seeing that I don't? What do I need to know? What do I need to consider? What adjustments need to be made? What are out options? They are seeking insight and perspective as they choose their next course of action.

There are hundreds of decisions and 20 different industries that must work together before a property actually closes – the very definition of integrated complexity. Sprinkle in the ever changing market, government and financial regulations, and the complexity compounds. A good coach makes a huge difference, because they have a perspective and wisdom that only up-to date current knowledge, real life experience, and the thousands of dedicated hours needed to have a high level of experience.

Example: A young family with 2 kids and 3rd on the way, needed a larger home. In order to buy their larger home, they needed the money from their current home. They were afraid to sell their home without knowing what they could purchase and when. They did not want to be rushed and forced to settle on a home just because of other's deadlines. They also did not want to waste money on rent and moving twice, but they felt they had no options. However, they actually had numerous options in this situation. Their skilled coach had several potential plays from their playlist gathered during the course of their long history.

1. They could make their new purchase contingent on the sale of their current home.
2. They could negotiate post possession that allows them to stay in the property until they identify and close on their next property. This is usually in the form of a lease.
3. They could structure a buy first, sell second

strategy using a variety of financing strategies. This could include alternative short terms financing or partial or full seller carry back.

4. We have even connected investors willing to purchase on behalf of the buyers (for a fee) and once their current property sells, they purchase from the investor.

This family had a clear understanding of the market thanks to a strong Wisdom Watson mindset. They also engaged their Accept or Change mindset that helped them accept that sellers were unlikely to choose an offer contingent on them finding a buyer for their home first when there were competing offers that were not contingent.

They relied on their "Expert Guidance Coaching" to help them review various alternatives and analyze the pros and cons of the various details. They opted for creative financing that would bridge their new purchase until they had funds from their sale. This put them in the best negotiating position when they made an offer on their new purchase.

To structure, negotiate, and implement that strategy successfully, they relied on their coach to help devise the best strategy for them, and carefully assemble experts in the 15 different industries involved in home selling. Their coach then created a detailed game plan for all the various players to follow so all the details and timelines were well executed.

Successful sellers look for skilled real estate guides/coaches to provide them with the best possible insights and wisdom to address the integrated complexity that is the journey of home selling.

# The Home Selling Journey

As you consider the big picture for your home selling journey you can see why most people start thinking about, and begin preparing to sell, months before they want to move.

Most everyone agrees that good marketing is important. What is often overlooked is the importance of conditioning the property first. Great photographs will not overcome a buyer's reaction to dirty baseboards, scuffed doors and walls, dead grass, broken fixtures etc... Likewise great photos and videos are hard to achieve until personal items are thinned and removed and all the rooms are decluttered.

Once de-cluttered and cleaned, the marketing preparation can begin. This phase includes soft staging or full staging, professional photography, videography, and drone video – think of this as the set design, lighting, and camera portion, of creating a box office hit. Before the director can step in and call "Action!" the sets need to be prepared, the script edited, actors hired, and costumes acquired. All of that occurs before any camera, lighting, or music work begins. We'll go into details about the Lights, Camera, Action Process to make it a Box Office Hit later in this book.

Experience shows that the work done in these early steps can result in a 10% or greater increase in what buyers are willing to pay. It may seem unlikely -- unless you have experienced helping a buyer looking at two homes with the exact same floor plan, same lot size, same year in the same neighborhood. One was well prepared, de-cluttered, sparkling clean (windows, carpets, yard, garage etc...). The other was worn, tired, cluttered. Guess which one got an offer quickly and guess what the ultimate price difference?

# The Preparation Process

Successful sellers are aware that today's buyers are driven by emotions and are influenced by current designs and trends as seen on many remodel and design shows. They are open to staging and designers advice and make the necessary changes to the interior and exterior required to capture the most interested buyers. Many buyers will be educated on the feature, function, benefits and value of similar houses, but it really comes down to how they feel about your property. You only get one chance to make a first impression. As mentioned in Mindset #2, "Failing to Prepare is Preparing to Fail." That's why focus on condition and preparation makes a difference.

Keep in mind it's not just getting an offer that means success. As mentioned earlier, one in five homes that receives an offer, never actually closes. So getting an offer is just the beginning – one of hundreds of steps that need to happen in a coordinated fashion that leads to being one of the four that closes and avoids being that one that fails.

Skilled real estate advisors, who do this every day are invaluable in helping you determine what repairs and improvements to make and, just as important, what won't provide a good return when selling. Most home sellers are surprised to know that many of the most impactful things cost little to no money. Let's take a closer look at the various steps in the marketing process.

**5** Stage and Prepare for Photos
**4** Clean, Repair, Declutter, Depersonalize
**3** Pre-Listing Inspection
**2** Room by Room Review
**1** Hire Your Real Estate Coach/Advisor

## The 70-30 Rule

Most people have 70% of the items in their home decorating and filling space. That leaves 30% actually showcasing the desirable features of the house. Look around your home right now…what do you think your ratio is? It is totally natural to surround yourself with all the things you love. But when selling a home, the ratio should be only 30% of your belongings and 70% actually showcasing the home features. This way you are highlighting the strengths of the house that will attract buyers.

This is our focus in the Home Selling Preparation phase – you are transforming space in your home that is filled with what you love, what identifies you and your family, what makes this "home" to you, and bringing the focus back to what we're marketing. We're marketing your house not your stuff.

To defend your equity and get you the highest offers from potential buyers we need to reduce your personal belongings. By reducing your personal family items to 30%, space is then opened up to welcome home buyers to envision their belongings and their family in that new space. If it sounds like you need shift your mindset to understand that its not your home anymore because it's the new buyers, you would be right.

# The Room By-Room Review

To start the process of reducing your personal items to 30% take notice of the things that are unique and specific to you, such as your interests, your hobbies, and your collections. I've worked with many people who have vibrant personalities, and its reflected in their home. When placing a house on the market it is best to go with subtle and neutral features over vibrant ones. Choosing neutrals will attract the most buyers because it allows each person to see themselves and their belongings in the space. That is the goal, to allow buyers to fall in love with a house by picturing themselves living there.

To simplify the process, a skilled professionals will conduct a Room-by-Room to help sellers. This plan prevents overwhelm and analysis paralysis by dividing the home into sections allowing you, the seller, to minimize your stress.

Take a look at a few before and after photos on pages 21-28 of some Room-by-Room results. You can see the impact that small, orchestrated changes can make.

There are three parts to the Room-By-Room Review:

- Viewing through the eye of the camera
- Pre-listing inspection peace of mind
- The emotional magic of soft staging

We go through the home with our sellers and look at each room and what's currently in it. Then we look at how to make the rooms stand out from the competition. Our sellers decide as we go through - what they are going to:

- Throw away?
- Give away? (This is a great time to help your favorite charity)
- Or Pack it away?

Doing this for each room opens up the space, allowing staging to create the desired effect that will appeal to buyers in each room.

## Through the Eye of the Camera

To reduce the overwhelm of preparing the home for sale, we use room-by-room process. In the first phase, it's about how to create a blank and neutral canvas to tell the story of your house. Search for the unintended distractions the camera will pick up and then consider what buyers will focus on in each room. It's helpful in this process to actually use a camera phone to capture the true picture of each room because it's been proven that our minds edit. When we hit the launch button for marketing, the online photos and videos will not edit. Even though I'm aware of it, my mind still edits unintentionally. It's important to have a good sense of which things draw people's attention, then determine if that focal point is the best marketing option. The result is a working plan that you can address in the time frame that best meets your needs.

This is a simple exercise you can do right now. Go to a room you think looks great and take a photo. See if the room looks as great in the photo or if you find yourself looking at something on the floor or something on a night stand versus

seeing the whole room. Look at it with an eye toward what should be moved to another location or removed completely.

## Pre-Listing Inspection Peace of Mind

Next, we examine what needs to be fixed, repaired, or enhanced. All of these things directly impact your ability to defend your equity -- the price a buyer is willing to pay. Why? Because a buyer's natural inclination is to exaggerate the repair or upgrade costs of every little flaw or repair. Some research findings show buyers estimate ten times more than what it would actually cost and their offer reflects that assumption. It is usually better to fix what you can up front. The more potential objections or concerns you remove, the more likely you are to receive full market value.

> *It's tempting to assume a buyer will overlook things because we have tolerated it for a while.*

Even the most conscientious homeowner can have things that need to be addressed. Knowing about it before it goes on the market means you can make an informed decision. Is it best to disclose defective items up front or make cost-effective repairs so they are a non-issue?

A word of caution here that speaks to Mindset #2. Its tempting to assume a buyer will overlook things because we have tolerated it for a while. In some markets that may be true. If it is not true, that assumption can be very costly. Its critical to understand market conditions. Is it a seller's market? Buyer's market? Or balanced market? The very same strategy may flourish when its a buyer's market, but fail in a seller's market. This is where the expertise and wisdom of an expert, leads, guides and protects sellers. Knowing the difference and to what extent buyers will tolerate less than ideal condition is one of the factors that explains why 1 of 5 contracts don't close. It also explains large variances in original list price vs. actual sale price. Also the price a property sold for is public knowledge. However, seller credits to the buyer to perform repairs is not public knowledge. So it may look like your neighbor sold for

$300K but actually only received $292K as they gave a credit to the buyer of $8K at the closing table.

Once you have the plan for what to fix, its time to determine who will fix it. You or a handyman? This gives you time to consider your time constraints and your ability to perform certain repairs or updates. Completing many repairs before marketing means there is no negotiation with the buyer on who will do the work or what type of fixtures or materials will be used.

> *For example, if after you are in contract, the buyer discovers that the roof needs repair, its not uncommon for the buyer to ask for a whole new roof (for a cost of $12K - $30K).*

For example, if after you are in contract, the buyer discovers that the roof needs repair, its not uncommon for the buyer to ask for a whole new roof (for a cost of $12K - $30K). One of our clients Dave and Judy had a rental property they were selling. Since they didn't live there, they didn't have detailed knowledge of the condition of the property.

The pre-listing home inspection uncovered a roof leak, A/C condensation line blockage, leaking sinks, drywall repairs and host of other items. It seemed like quite a bit. But when grouped together by trade: roofer, handyman, A/C it was quite manageable. All but the roof and AC, were easily fixed by a handyman. If they were requested to be fixed by the buyer after contract, the buyer could require even the smallest of repairs be completed by licensed vendors.

That increases the cost significantly for a couple reasons. One reason is the more specialists required, the more trip charges there are ($50-$125). Second, since many handymen work by the hour, they can install ceiling fans, microwaves, electrical outlets, unclog a sink, repair drywall and paint and charge for 3 or 4 hours. Imagine the fees for a plumber, painter, and electrician for 1 or 2 items. In this case, Dave

# Example Repair List - 123 Main Street

**Preliminary Staging**
- Pack all personal photos
- Living room-move white table from entry into corner of living room
- Remove rug
- Remove all stuffed animals and minimize pet toys
- Kitchen-remove magnets from refrigerator and minimize items on the counters
- TV room-move sofa under window, pack and store personal property
- Office-pack unused items and tidy up desk areas
- Patio- remove cover from table and chair set

**REPAIRS/TO-DO**

**Exterior of home**
- Hose down or power wash exterior including fascia board and eaves
- Wash and spray paint security screen door
- Replace white motion light at exterior of garage
- Replace damaged ceiling fan in garage with a white light
- Paint front and north side fencing (dark brown)
- Install dark brown mulch in planter beds
- Increase water in front yard to green up grass
- Install outlet cover at west side of garage
- Paint rear patio ceiling by electrical panel (white)

**Interior of home**
- Paint exterior of front door
- Caulk master bathroom shower
- Clean track of sliding glass door so that it slides easier
- Install updated light fixtures in bathroom

**Items to Purchase**
- White exterior light for garage
- White interior light to replace damaged ceiling fan (garage)
- Ceiling fan (master bedroom)
- Bathroom light fixture
- Mulch for planter beds
- Exterior cover for electrical outlet

Schedule handyman that we recommended to help with repairs
Schedule professional cleaning company that we recommended

and Judy had a roofer repair not just the leak but they also did a full roof inspection and performed maintenance to the flashings, and areas that are most likely to fail. For $500 they provided a two-year roof certification. So the buyer received a clean bill of health from a licensed roofer along with a 2 year warranty for that roof. If they had not remedied the roof first, what are the chances the buyer would have asked for new roof (this roof was 19 years old)? Even with a $350 pre-listing home inspection fee, Dave and Judy attribute a savings of $15,000 because they knew what the issues were, they had skilled guidance on what and how to manage the repairs, and they had reliable quality vendors to perform the repairs timely and cost effectively.

Finally if there are items that you choose not to fix, you then disclose those items on the seller's disclosure statement. Disclosing up front reduces the chances of the buyer's home inspector making a mountain out of a molehill. The last thing you want for the buyer is to feel uneasy about the condition of the home. Letting buyers know up front builds trust and avoids the "surprise" factor. The "surprise factor" is when the buyer wonders, "What else did they not tell me?" That can drastically undermine the process. Yep you guessed it... Another reason 1 of 5 contracts do not close.

## Clean – Repair – De-Clutter – Depersonalize

Once the Pre-Listing Inspection and the Room-By-Room Review are completed, you have a master plan on what to do to prepare your house for the market. A list of trusted vendors who specialize in everything from deep cleaning to home repairs would be very helpful.

This is a time to remember when everything is done right you can expect to sell your home in 30 days or less. It's worth the preparation, so why not get packing now when everything is less hectic than it will be once you're under contract for the sale.

The best advice for every seller, is to have your home immaculate and white glove clean. Buyers believe clean equals well maintained. Dirty homes can trigger the feeling of lack of care and unattended and will start searching for the homes weaknesses. Experience shows it best to do whatever it takes to make it feel like Mr. and Mrs. Clean live here. This includes the most overlooked items when preparing a house for sale, the windows!

Remember, professional photographers will be shooting through the windows to bring the outdoors in and those windows must sparkle! Even if you have to hire a window washer.

**As for repairs, your real estate coach/advisor will help you:**

- Determine what must be done based on your specific situation
- What makes financial sense to take care of
- What to disclose and let the next owner determine how to handle.

## The Marketing Process

The Home Selling Journey is made up of the Preparation process to defend your equity while the Marketing process is a comprehensive strategy to have your home attract buyers willing to pay the highest price with the most desirable terms.

### THE MARKETING PROCESS

- Show Time
- Full Launch Marketing
- Coming Soon Marketing
- Pinpoint Pricing
- Staging and Photo Preparation

## The Emotional Magic of Soft Staging

The third, and final part of the Room-By-Room review is creating an emotional attraction to the house. This is what all potential buyers are looking for; to feel the excitement of this is home. To help visually attract home buyers, trained professionals use a technique called soft staging. The best way to explain soft staging is taking what is available in the home (or what may be stored in the professional's staging warehouse). The best way to explain soft staging is taking what is available in the home (or what we have stored in our staging warehouse) and creating vignettes that sell the lifestyle potential buyers are wishing to lead. Buying is an emotional process. Bring emotional and magnetic attraction to each room, so buyers "feel at home".

Your home can subliminally become more attractive to buyers with just a few strategically placed items. This is why we suggest you team with a real estate advisor that is a marketing expert rather than an traditional agent. When you hire a marketing expert before your home is placed on the market, they will apply proven strategies to market it to sell quickly and just as important to sell for top and just as important to sell for top dollar.

A picture is worth a thousand words. Take a look at examples of how the Room-By-Room Review and Soft Staging can make your house more visually attractive to potential buyers.

Master bedroom before

MINDSET SECRETS FOR HOMES SELLERS

Master bedroom after

## Solids for School Pictures and Bedrooms

Do you remember when you were a kid and your parents prepared you for picture day at school? Or when you had a family photograph? What's the first thing a photographer tells you when preparing for these events? To wear solid colors! Why? Because solids will "stand out" in the photo better then prints and patterns. As the subject of a photograph we look best when we wear solid color, and the same is true for each room in your house.

A lot of times homeowners will have bedspreads with patterns and prints and it's distracting and sometimes can distract buyers. A dynamic change can happen in a room when you take a neutral colored bedspread that is complimentary with the room paint color. It can be a very inexpensive purchase that will highlight the room and make it stand out. It is just like when you see your childhood school picture and you're wearing that solid shirt, you show well, and that is the same for well-staged room.

When selling your home, it becomes a house and it is no longer about what you like. You are presenting the house as a product and in the master bedroom the goal is to make it feel like a relaxing retreat. Need a visual? Just imagine a five-star hotel room and if you're not sure, Google any of the major hotel chains. Hilton, Holiday Inn, etc. and you can check out their room photos online. Those nice hotel rooms have solid colored bedspreads that look clean and crisp. In our own homes our bedspreads can be comfy and we love them because they're comfortable but worn. But this can cause your buyer to subliminally equate worn with dirty. Buyers are looking to buy a "new home" with a "fresh start"; presenting your home as crisp and clean is always a winner. Create the effect of walking into a hotel room; "Ahhhh, I can relax here, this is my sanctuary, this is tranquil, and inviting." It's a simple tip that has a huge impact when the camera is marrying the look of the room to the emotion created in the potential buyer.

Some of the basics to consider for bedspreads are white (but not when you have white walls), beige, navy, grey and a punch of color like blue or green in kid's or guest rooms. The master bedroom bed should have four pillows stacked two and two. For added excellence add an accent pillow or two. The key here is the bedspreads usually don't have to be expensive – you can pick up a full, queen or king sets with shams, pillows, and a dust ruffle for $75 at Ross, TJ Maxx or Target. Trust me, it's $75 well spent and the really nice thing once you successfully sell your house, you get to take it to your new home.

## Take Me Away Calgon…

Bathrooms even when dated are one of the most important rooms in the house. Absolutely critical for a good impression is they must be clean, not just tidy but CLEAN! Nothing derails a buyer faster than a bathroom that feels grungy!

Its common for homes that have not been updated, to have colors, fixtures or stains that are undesirable to buyers. To minimize the impact (without the cost of a remodel) go to the hotel formula where white = clean, fresh, and relaxing.

In the bathroom featured here you can see there was a lot going on: a patterned shower curtain, bath rugs, various artwork, personal hygiene items on the countertop (which screams

Bathroom before

Bathroom after

26 BETH REBENSTORF

not enough counter space!) The after photo is an example of soft staging. By eliminating items, toning patterns and colors down with a crisp white cloth shower curtain and luxurious white towels (along with something green, something living, something inviting) it created a less frenzied, more tranquil feeling. And again… no matter what, it must be clean!

Did you notice the delicate orchid on the back of the toilet? I bet you did. It adds a pop of color and it also serves another purpose, which is to draw buyers into the room. For about $400 the tub could have be painted white with special acrylic paint. However, since the tile border, accents and soap holders were colored, it was determined the $400 cold be better spent elsewhere … and the white shower curtain did a better job of toning things down and improving the attractiveness in photos.

The soft staging you see is not expensive –knowing what to buy and how to pull it together to get the desired effect. The result for this family was multiple offers and top dollar for this home, quickly and with compassion.

With an experienced real estate guide, you get the benefit of know-how about the tips, tricks, and secrets to making your home look its best, so it appeals to buyers. You get protection from spending money on things that may not yield enough of a return to make it worthwhile. More importantly you get this insight when you need it most - BEFORE your home is on the market.

Have you ever seen a house not sell come back on the market weeks or months later? Even then, after updates, repairs, and staging, buyers are keenly aware that it did not sell previously and they assume the worst … "What is wrong with it?" The old photos are there for all buyers to see – (no they do NOT go away – they stay available on the internet sites). Its very difficult to un-see what's already been seen.

As you are beginning to understand, preparation matters big time. Experience shows that a home that has been properly prepared, staged, and photographed typically sells at 10% more than others that skip these steps.

## Green - the Color for Money and Life

Another exceptional tip is the power of having something green or simulated living in several rooms of the house. If you don't have a green thumb, artificial plants are great. When artificial plants don't fit you, it could be as simple as a green vase or some other item that's green. In this bathroom, de-cluttering created a nice blank canvas. To make sure the environment didn't feel sterile, a simple green silk plant or some fresh flowers add a lot on photography day.

Now that you know this tip, the next time you're in a staged home, at department stores or other decorated places you'll likely notice that there's always something green.

As-is bathroom prior to staging and decluttering personal items.

Staged, lit an decluttered; this bathroom is worthy of a hotel rating now.

Some other elements from nature are seashells or twine balls that people may notice and subliminally connect as living items. Knowing how to use these subtle vignettes and strategically positioning inexpensive accessories are the kind of things a skilled expert will take the time to include.

# It's Show time – Lights, Lights, and More Lights

The final soft staging tip is to check all your lighting. Make sure that you have the highest wattage light bulbs in all your lighting. All lights should be plugged in and working. Buyers are naturally attracted to brightness; if you've watched any home TV shows, you've heard the compliment of "the home is light and airy." Create the feeling of sunlight because people tend to feel happier when there is light. If you have any rooms that are dark because of the angle of the sun or because of trees, let the wattage of the light bulbs work for your house. Bring the outdoors in and create that really bright feeling. In this example by correcting the lighting it emphasized the beautiful crown molding on the ceiling. Its completely missed in the dark photo.

The den/office space after staging.

Think of going to the theater, or filming for a movie. Stage lighting is bright so the audience can see the actors. The same effect needs to be created in your house. This is show time for your house so the goal is to create the atmosphere where your house shines its very best!

Top; The den/office space prior to staging and setting the lights.

One of the things that surprises many clients, is the immense difference experience in the preparation stage makes. Its tempting to skip over that whole phase to rush to market but the only person that harms is the seller. **A trusted advisor, committed to lead, guide, and protect a seller's best interests will take the time and effort to protect the extra equity for their seller.** Remember Mindset #3? Successful sellers have a deep respect for the thousand of hours and dollars invested to master any craft, so they seek expert advice. There is a reason that 5% of all real estate agents represent 95% of all the sold homes.

Before: Declutter Desperation

After: Clean, bright and spacious

# Pictures and Videos are Key

Outdoor living space After

Outdoor living space before

**PHOTOS** In addition to using the photos captured on the phone camera before professional photos to create the conditioning action list, they are also used for our Silent Market. This is our list of buyers interested in similar properties. We notify our list of Silent Market buyers about coming soon properties before they hit the market.

**INTERIOR VIDEO** An interior video walks a buyer through the home to get great understanding of the "flow" of a home. Many times when looking at only photos, buyers scratch their head and ponder a photo of a room trying to figure out, where it is in relation to the other rooms. Does that door go the garage? Laundry? Pantry? Hallway? Bathroom? Den? How big is the closet? Are there 2 closets? It can provide clarity on size of rooms and closets, views from windows, how the tile, carpet, wood flooring connect. Its as close to walking through the home as possible without being there.

**EXTERIOR DRONE VIDEO** An exterior drone video highlights the home, yard, location, community amenities and neighborhood in a way photos simply can't. Is the property near a park, golf course, lake? Is there space for RV parking? Is there room for a pool or play equipment? How close are the neighbors? Where is the community pool? These are questions that drone video answers beautifully for buyers, and will keep that property on the "show" list.

# Lifestyle and Views = Money Shots

The goal of a marketing expert is to skillfully craft the story to appeal to the next owner. Selecting the best angle, views, quality and sequence for photos and videos all make a difference in how the audience (buyers) respond.

- How does this house compare to others buyers will view?
- What are this house's strengths?
- How do we minimize any weaknesses?
- What is the best strategy to compete?

It's important to differentiate between potential buyer objections which can be handled, and the property condition, which can not changed, but can be minimized.

For example, if you have a house that has a small yard, there's nothing that can be done to change that. You would however, highlight the stress-free, low maintenance of a smaller yard

and the positives of a lifestyle with more time to do things you love rather than being tied to time intensive high maintenance yard work. Target each house to appeal to the person who will appreciate its features versus someone who won't.

When you have a view whether mountains, greenbelt, golf course, city lights or gorgeous back yard oasis...it is a huge selling feature to buyers. An experienced real estate guide will help you highlight and focus on those features. This is what we call the money shot!

When you are selling a property whether it's a house, a townhouse, a condominium or a villa.... You are selling a dream! Buyers are dreaming about the memories they will make, the good times they will have and the enjoyment they will gain by living there.

It's important from a marketing perspective to understand when is the best time for prospective buyers to see your property. If your property gets sunset views you'd like to make sure potential buyers experience that.

# Making Your Home a Box Office Hit Lights, Camera, Action!

What makes a blockbuster hit movie? Why is one movie so well received or over another? It's never one single thing. It's the combination of many things at the right time that garner audience response.

In the beginning a box office hit is nothing more than a story or script (your house.) The journey to box office hit requires, vision, planning, preparation, filming, editing, and marketing.

As the producer/director for each house "launch", we look at everything through a lens with the viewer (buyer) in mind and focus on how to professionally present each house as a Box Office Hit. We build the scene, edit the script, set the stage, make sure everyone looks their best with lighting and make-up. We then direct and capture it all on film. After final editing, the public needs to know about it. Even better, they should eagerly anticipate it! Cue the teasers, trailer, and sneak peaks (coming soon signs, internet marketing, single property websites, info box flyers, open house invites, silent market invites...)

When there is an anticipated "release date", the interest builds and grows. People talk about it and make plans to see it. On launch day, the red carpet is rolled out for the much anticipated hit! The goal is multiple offers in the first week; especially in a strong seller's market.

That's how sellers get the most amount of money with the

> *When there is an anticipated "release date", the interest builds and grows. People talk about it and make plans to see it. On launch day, the red carpet is rolled out for the much anticipated hit!*

least amount of stress. Which is most likely to generate multiple offers? A single showing or buyers lined up to view your house.

A lot of time has been spent on the planning phase for a reason -- It's absolutely critical! Everything hinges on how the buyer responds to the photos, video, and personal tours! So where do box office flops go wrong? What's the best way for you to avoid being 1 of the 5 that does not sell? By now you understand the importance of all 3 Mindsets successful sellers share. Missing one of them can and does impact the outcome.

# Pinpoint Pricing – How Important is it Really?

Once you've completed everything you can to create a perception of high value, its time for your next and **MOST IMPORTANT** decision. This one singular crucial decision – over all other decisions will determine success or failure. There are a variety of pricing strategies. One is not better or worse than another.... Except when applied in market conditions where it will fail or under perform. Assuming "the one" strategy will work in all circumstances is like a doctor prescribing only one treatment.

Using the same strategy that worked 10 years, or 10 months ago can be very dangerous. Ignoring property condition, buyer preferences, market conditions, local and neighborhood issues, and financing conditions is like a doctor overlooking things that make for good and healthy outcomes.

The best doctors consider root cause and symptoms combined with quality of outcome and financial viability. Plastic surgery may be the best option for one patient, and simply not viable for another – for financial, physical, or personal reasons. Similarly a house may be in need of a brand new roof, the pool may need significant repairs to get the highest sale price. Will a $20K new roof result in an additional $30K $20K or 10K offer price? What will a $4K pool upgrade result in? Does the homeowner have the money to invest in updates? How much stress are they willing or able to handle? Is it worth it? Or is it better to adjust with price?

## There Is Only ONE Reason a House Does Not Sell!

Want to guess what that is? The ONLY reason a house becomes 1 of the 5 that does not sell is because the wrong pricing strategy for current conditions was chosen. The right price makes ALL the difference. Knowing how to arrive at that right price requires considering a variety of different factors.

- LOCATION
- CONDITION OF PROPERTY
- FAIR MARKET VALUE
- SUPPLY & DEMAND
- ECONOMIC TRENDS
- NEW CONSTRUCTION
- DISTRESSED PROPERTIES

Overlooking some or even one of those factors means missing information that affects success or failure.

Its tempting to make assumptions that are not accurate. Like since the neighboring property sold for $300,000, mine will too! Only that was 14 months ago. By itself the logic seems reasonable. However, a series of other factors must also be applied. That neighboring property may have been larger, had a larger lot, extra garage, or better location. Or perhaps one home was upgraded and the other home is in original condition. Or 14 months ago, inventory was very low. Or only 5 homes sold in that neighborhood in the entire year vs. now there 6 currently for sale. Or a six-lane highway was announced less than $1/2$ a mile from the neighborhood. There are literally thousands of factors to consider when determining initial price. This is where experience is absolutely critical. There is no shortcut to gaining the deep experience and breadth of knowledge that guides this make-or-break decision.

# There is Only One Chance for Maximum Interest. After the Initial Launch the Opportunity Windows Only Closes

**The pricing strategy decision is the single most critical decision because it's the most damaging to a seller if its flawed.** No other decision is more harmful than the wrong price for current conditions. Why? Because it is only one decision.  In preparation, staging, marketing, there are hundreds of decisions, so being off a bit is less impactful - more forgiving. The wrong price however is unforgiving. Its "on" or "off" with very little in between.

Once your home goes live to the public with the price, there is no going back. The launch is the opening of your marketing window. It is wide open only once. After that, your window is only closing, closing, closing. There is no opportunity for another launch. That's why launching like a box office hit is so essential. Once reviews are out, the first impression has occurred. There is no 2nd chance for another first impression.

Which situation is most likely to result in the highest price? The house that had lots of showings immediately after going live, or the house that has been on the market for weeks or months with several price reductions?  The latter is a death nail for getting the highest price. The longer a home is on the market the lower the eventual price. As a matter of fact, we love it when a neighbor overprices their home because it just helps appropriately priced homes sell faster and for more money.

# Type of Markets and What that Means

### Balanced Market

A balanced market is when supply and demand are fairly equal. The number of home buyers is about the same as the number of home sellers. Usually that's 4-6 months supply of inventory depending your area and market.

To determine the monthly supply, take the number of homes currently available and divide by the number of homes that sold last month (or the average of what sold the last 3 months).

### Sellers Market

A seller's market is when demand is higher than supply. Buyers are competing with other buyers for sellers to accept their offer, which drives up price and reduces the selling time. This means buyers will spend more to get what they want, especially if the property condition is excellent. These conditions often trigger bidding wars, which are ideal for sellers to get the highest price and desired terms.

**The Impact of Monthly Housing Inventory on Home Prices**

# Buyers Market

A buyers market is when supply is higher than demand. Sellers compete to attract buyers. Circumstances are ideal for buyers. Price is a key determining factor, along with other incentives from the seller to the buyer. Since buyers have so many options, it is common for buyers to receive concessions from the seller such as:

- Lower price
- Updates or repairs (new roof, paint, update flooring, fix pool....)
- Pay all or some of buyer's closing costs
- Allow seller to have possession for a period of time after purchase for seller to find next home or move out

Its important to keep in mind, while one segment of the market may be a seller's market, another may be a buyer's market. For instance, there was a period of time in Arizona where the luxury market had a 2-4 year supply of inventory, it was a buyer's market, pressuring sellers to lower prices if they wanted to sell.

At the very same time, anything under $300K that was in reasonable condition was rarely on the market for more than two-weeks. It was a strong buyer's market. Multiples offers were common and price and terms being offered to sellers were generous and creative. It was a challenge for buyers to get their offer accepted.

# Market Value – the Start Point for All Decisions

## Market Value

Market value is the assumption that all other decisions are based on. Banks determine the amount they will finance for the buyer based on a percentage of appraised value. Buyers make their offer based on what they believe market value to be. Buyers, agents and appraisers rely on the same data to determine current market value.

Because market value is the start point for all decisions, its imperative the market value assumption is accurate. If it is flawed, all decisions based on it are likewise flawed.

Buyers may offer too little. Reaching agreement when the buyer believes sellers are "crazy" and want too much and sellers are "insulted" and believe buyer is stealing from them does not bode well. Either the buyers must adjust their assumption to increase their offer or the seller must adjust their assumption and agree to accept a lower price.

| Asking price in relation to market value | % Of potential buyers who will look at property |
|---|---|
| +15% | 10% |
| +10% | 30% |
| MARKET VALUE | 60% |
| -10% | 75% |
| -15% | 90% |

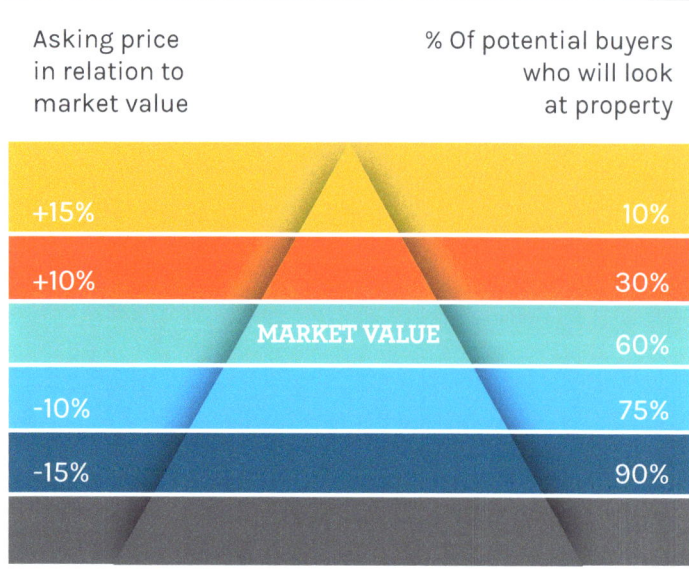

Buyers may also offer too much which may seem a good thing for the seller. Until the buyer's loan is denied because the appraised value is less than the purchase price. At that point there are 3 options:

1. Buyer agrees to overpay and come in with the difference in cash (as the lender will not finance the difference)
2. Seller and buyer agree on a reduced price
3. Buyer cancels

You kill the deal?

What about when the seller's assumption of value is off? If a property is listed too high, fewer buyers actually know about it or see it. If its priced 15% above market value only 10-30% of buyers will actually see an overpriced property. Buyers are well educated and have access to all the information and data that appraisers, lenders, and agents use to determine fair market value.

> *"You do what you do, When you know what you know, When you know different, You do different"*
>
> — Oprah Winfrey

If a buyer does make an offer and the seller's market value assumption is flawed often the seller will counter to get closer to perceived value. If the buyers have a skilled negotiator guiding them, they may agree to the overpriced amount knowing that the appraisal will not support that value, At that point the buyer can cancel the contract and their earnest money refunded to them (per AZ's Dept. of Real Estate 2018 purchase contract) unless agreed to otherwise.

Most often sellers begrudgingly agree to meet the appraisal value. If their assumption of market value were accurate in the beginning, they would have made different decisions. Not only would they have avoided frustration and disappointment, they may have attracted a different buyer, or multiple buyers. I love what Oprah Winfrey said,

# Appraisals and How They Can Affect Sellers

### FEAR – False Evidence Appearing Real

Sometimes sellers are resolute and refuse to accept what they cannot change. That's what we call **FEAR** – False Evidence Appearing Real. Its similar to **FOMO** (Fear of Missing Out which we discuss in the next section)

It's understandable that sellers do not want to leave money on the table, and that buyers do not want to overpay.

**False Evidence Appearing Real**

They want to believe another buyer will a) agree to a higher price and b) that a new appraisal will be higher. A couple things are important to understand in these circumstances:

1. **FHA appraisals stay with property for 90 days** If its FHA financing (95% of all loans) the appraisal stays with the property for 90 days regardless of who the next buyer is. So unless the next buyer is cash, conventional, or private financing, the appraisal value will not change. Also an appraisal is not a requirement for a cash buyer, but the cash buyer has the right and often does have it appraised. It's a risky roll of the dice to rely on a getting a better offer that is cash or conventional financing in the homes that a new appraisal will be higher.

2. **Appraisal Appeal Process** Although appraisers use standard procedures, formulas, and algorithms to arrive at their value, they are human and do make mistakes. Its not common but it does occur. The appeal process is designed to remedy mistakes, but only if evidence is provided to support it. An experienced real estate agent will help you with this process.

Two of the most common reasons an appraisal is adjusted are:

**Missing Comps or Non Comparables** – If recently sold comparable properties (Comps) were not used or properties that are not comparable were used it could be grounds for appeal. Lets say a home down the street with the same number of bedrooms and bathrooms as your home; and with a similar number of rooms and square footage sold within the last 90 days, but was not included in the appraisal. That could be grounds for an appeal (if it in fact increased the overall value.)

Or if a non-comparable home 3 streets over that does not have a pool, has 1 less bedroom, 2 fewer bathrooms was used as a comparable. It may be acceptable as ground for appeal especially if an actual comparable was available but omitted.

**Home Improvements Omitted or Other Errors** — Appraisers research as much as possible to prepared prior to the on-site inspection. Part of that research is in public records, which may not be accurate. Your home may have an addition that is not reflected. Or there was a data entry error in number of bedrooms, bathrooms, year built, lot size or square footage. An appraiser will generally measure and map the home, but may not measure the yard. So there could be errors that need to be corrected that would adjust the outcome.

*Your assumption, and the truth, dine at totally separate tables.*

Likewise their on-site visit is the best way to determine if hardwood floors were recently installed or that the kitchen and all bathrooms were extensively remodeled. Or without your receipts they would not know about the $20K 6 month old roof. If those items were missed, they can be corrected and a new value calculated.

The more objective you are, the more accurate your data assumptions will be. The more accurate (and complete) your data analysis and interpretation, the more reliable your market value assumption – which is what all your decisions are based on. So an accurate, reliable market value assumption leads to better decisions.

Many a seller regrets letting what they "want the market to be" override what the market actually is. It's the single most harmful error, because every decision is based on what a seller believes (rightly or wrongly) market value is. Consider the different conclusion sellers and buyers reach about a $370K offer when the market value assumption is $400K vs. $370K. Its tempting to conclude that the impact is insignificant. However, actual results show a very different conclusion.

Experience (and data) show the longer a property is on the market, the lower the sale price. If buyers think no one else is interested in the property, they feel comfortable offering less or waiting to see if there are better options. They also think something is wrong with the property. If a buyer's budget is $370K, they may never even know about the overpriced $400K listing. Or they may come across it but overlook it in favor of market priced properties.

# Pricing Strategies

**Price at Market Value or Price Higher...** Many sellers share with me that they want to price their property higher than market value because they believe a buyer will offer below market value if its priced properly... Right at market value. The evidence does not support that. In fact the opposite is true.

Consider bank-owned/foreclosed properties. Many buyers believe foreclosures are automatically a "great" deal - that they can pick them up for under market value. The fact that the property was foreclosed is not what determines whether a seller (in this case the bank) is willing to sell for under market. Market conditions determine that. Its common to see banks use an effective "auction" tactic. This where they price a property below market value and accept "bids". All the interested parties are then contacted and informed that the seller (the bank) has multiple offers. Any buyers still interested can adjust their offer higher if they want to win the bid. Guest what happens? The property sells for well above the original list price and very often above market value! That's right! Its human nature during a bidding war that buyers fear they will miss out on the "great" deal. The price goes higher and higher because of **FOMO — Fear Of Missing Out!**

Pricing higher does not attract the attention that triggers FOMO. In fact pricing too high, means it sits on the market, and offers that finally do come in are lower than homes properly priced.

There are certain market conditions, certain types of properties, or certain neighborhoods where the strategy of pricing above market is an effective and wise strategy. In a hot, hot, hot market where prices are clearly increasing, when

inventory is very low and buyers have few options, or highly desirable neighborhoods that rarely see a property for sale.

We discussed previously that it's the proper use of a strategy in the right market conditions that matter—not the strategy itself.

# Multiple Offers

**Multiple Offers – Best Chance for Highest Price** No matter what the market conditions are, having more than one offer- even if one is a "low ball" investor offer, will exponentially increase your chances of getting the highest price the market will bear. The buyer will not know the price or terms of any other offers you received. All they know is someone else might get the home they want. That's the strongest negotiating position you can have.

Timing plays a critical role on multiple offers. The longer a property is on the market, the less likely it will attract more than one offer. Experience shows the most likely time a property will receive multiple offers is in the first 7-10 days after initial launch.

| Buyer | Offer Price | Concessions Paid by Seller | Home Warranty | Net Offer | Finance Type | Close Date | Down Payment | Contingent on Selling Property | Washer, Dryer, Fridge? |
|---|---|---|---|---|---|---|---|---|---|
| 1 | 390,000 | 4,000 | 375 | 385,625 | Conventional | 29-Sep | 3,000 | No | Yes |
| 2 | 399,000 | 0 | 0 | 399,000 | Conventional | 17-Oct | 5,000 | No | Yes |
| 3 | 405,000 | 6,500 | 250 | 398,250 | FHA | 29-Sep | 1,500 | Yes | Yes |

Why? Back to **FOMO** - Fear Of Missing Out. Most buyers are choosing a home for emotional reasons. FOMO is very real. If you have heard stories about red hot seller markets like California, you've heard about properties going for $100k -$200k and even higher than list price! In our Arizona market, we have experienced all the cycles. When it's a seller's market (low supply, high demand) conditions are ripe for multiple offers and FOMO is high.

Understanding what does and does not matter when determining market value can help avoid succumbing to FEAR (False Evidence Appearing Real.) Neutralizing FEAR means making better decisions at the most important time - at the launch when interest is at its all time high.

Remember buyer interest only decreases with time. It does not increase. Better decisions at launch increase your chances of multiple offers. Multiple offers increase the likelihood of the highest price. An accurate market value leads to choosing effective pricing strategy and a wise negotiation strategy when reviewing offers.

## Things That Trigger More Than One Offer –

There are ideal conditions for getting more than one offer. Some you have no control over and some you do.

### Things Within Your Control

- Your property shows extremely well- clean, de-cluttered, well staged,

- Photos and videos show your property to its full advantage

- Buyers perceive your property as the "10" property compared other similar properties that have sold or are available.

- Many buyers view your property in the first 10 days on the market.

- There are no major repair issues or obvious blemishes.

- You determined your initial price based on accurate realistic market data.

- You choose a skilled guide and negotiator to represent you and your property. They share what will serve your interests and they keep confidential what will not serve you.

### Things Not In Your Control

- It's a buyer's market
- The location of your property
- How much a buyer can afford
- The value an appraiser assigns

# Things That **DO** Matter to Market Value

- Sale price within 90 days similar homes, of similar age, size,
- Recently sold properties of similar size, age, amenities, and in same neighborhood
- The amount of time similar homes in the neighborhood sold
- Price trends of homes in the neighborhood
- The supply of inventory of similar homes in the neighborhood
- The home's overall condition and upgrades compared to sold including age of roof, condition of exterior and interior
- The home's configuration, including bedrooms, bathrooms, garage
- Age and condition of mechanical, A/C, heat pump, solar panels, water heater, plumbing, electrical
- Recent home improvements including flooring, kitchen, bathrooms lighting fixtures, plumbing fixtures
- Size of the home's lot compared to other homes in the neighborhood
- Backyard conditions and amenities (pool, spa, BBQ, fire pit, water features hardscaping…)
- Lot location, mountain, city, golf, lake views, waterfront, backs to mountain or preserve, next to greenbelt, backs to busy street, corner…
- Type of community – gated, lake, golf course, rec center, clubhouse…
- Zoning of neighboring properties
- A home's uniqueness ("unique" is often a negative)

## Things That *DO NOT* Matter to Market Value

- How much the seller paid originally
- How much the seller "needs" for something else (another property, trip around the world, debt...)
- How much the seller paid for "upgrades"
- Similar house sold for $200sf so my house should get $200 x my square footage - Sorry... If only it were so simple! Might be coincidence that it sometimes it works out that way, but it does not work that way.
- You absolutely love your house and put lots of creative energy and love into it (remember we are all different and you are selling space not your personal preferences)

# 10/10 Rule of Showings

10/10 Rule  I learned this rule from my friend Cindy Flowers, a long time fabulous Arizona agent who has helped thousands of families during her 30 year career. While there are exceptions to every "rule", in my experience this 10/10 rule is a really good rule of thumb.  Here is the rule:

## 10/10 RULE

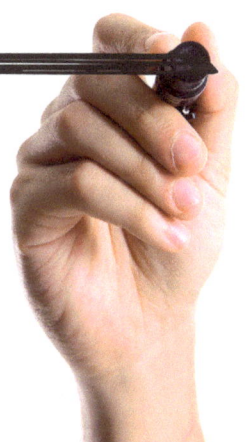

1. If your home is on the market for 10 days and you don't have 10 showings —you are over priced.

2. If your home does have 10 showings in the first 10 days and you don't have an offer—you are over priced.

## 10/10 Rule Part 1
If your home is on the market for 10 days and you don't have 10 showings —you are over priced.

## 10/10 Rule Part 2
If your home does have 10 showings in the first 10 days and you don't have an offer—you are over priced.

This brings us back mindset #2 – Accept what can't be changed. The 10/10 rule helps sellers accept what the market is saying. All the data shows that the closer to market value, the quicker you will receive an offer … and likewise the further away from market, the longer it will take to receive an offer. And the longer a property has been on the market the less valuable buyers perceive it. They wonder what's wrong with it, which is reflected in their offer price. There are no do-overs on first impressions, making a price adjustment should occur sooner rather than later.

Now if it is buyer's market with say a 6-10 month supply of available homes, the 10 days might adjust to say 30 days. The important concept is to choose your pricing strategy based on objective market value, buyer perception of property condition, and current market conditions. If any of those assumptions are off, your conclusions are off and offer price and timing are negatively impacted.

# Top 10 Seller Mistakes

**01** — Making Emotional Decisions

**02** — Ignoring Market Data and Market Feedback

**03** — Thinking Buyers will Overlook Poor Conditions

**04** — Sharing Too Much with Buyers
*(Less is More and More Can be Harmful)*

**05** — Assigning an inflated value to upgrades

**06** — Too many restrictions on showing

**07** — Thinking "staging" does not make a difference

**08** — Spending money on things that don't yield a return

**09** — Thinking data is the same as skillfully applying data

**10** — Not accepting what can't be changed

# What about iBuyers? Online Instant Offers?

**i**Buyers are companies that will make an offer to buy a property at a "convenience" price through online systems. The "i" in iBuyer comes from "instant, internet" offer.

These companies use technology platforms and Automated Valuation Models (AVMs) to estimate the property's value to make an offer without seeing the property and usually respond with an offer in 1-4 days. Then they turn it around and sell it within 30-60 days for a small profit.

There is no shortage of technology advances. But, the fact is, real estate transactions are more complex and challenging than ever before.

iBuyers will offer to purchase homes directly from sellers at a price that considers the CONVENIENCE factors of:

*Certainty – they buy with cash, so no loan contingencies*

*Closing Date Choice – sellers can select the closing date of their choice (usually with 5-60 days)*

*Convenience – no showings, staging, open houses, preparation, or repairs*

iBuyers are professional investors with a business model that relies on high volume and quick turn around. They do not seek out distressed properties that require a lot of work and they do not operate in all markets. They each have specific buying criteria specific to the markets area and prefer properties in good condition that need minimal investment to put back on the market for a quick resell. Typically there is a maximum price limit and age of the home. In the Phoenix area it is limited to homes built after 1960.

There are several common exclusions including:

- **Pre-fabricated/manufactured/mobile homes**
- **Lot size greater than an acre (currently)**
- **Located in a flood zone**
- **Homes with non-permitted additions, significant foundation issues, solar leases, polybutylene plumbing**
- **Distressed property or no clear title**
- **No lease at the time of closing**

iBuyer "convenience" fees are typically between 6% -8% and as high as 14%, And the offer price is usually lower than what the property might realize when listed on MLS. And sellers still have to pay closing costs and either make repairs or reduce the offer price to cover repairs.

The majority of sellers want to get maximum value. However, sometimes the iBuyer convenience offer is a good option. Its important to know that sellers can still be represented by a real estate expert they trust to guide them through the process.

Much like in new construction where new build estate agents only represent the seller, iBuyer agents only represent the iBuyer. Just as it's important that new build buyers have their own agent advocating and protecting them, it's important that sellers have someone they trust to lead, guide, and protect them throughout the process - especially if they choose an iBuyer offer.

It is a common practice for us to help sellers consider offers from iBuyers. In fact, having a professional involved often IMPROVES the offer from instant offer companies because:

1. They know the real estate professional will provide the seller with data and interpretation of current market value. They know they are competing with other iBuyers, investors, and traditional buyers which means it is less likely they will "lowball" the value.

2. They know the professional has actually seen the property, knows the condition, the market, the neighborhood - all the niche details that an automated value algorithm is unable to consider.

3. They know the real estate professional will represent the seller's interests when it comes to repair requests. Most of the time, iBuyers request a list of repairs or instead of repairs they want a reduction in price. Knowing which repairs are reasonable, and accurate costs for the requested repairs can save sellers a significant amount of money.

4. When the seller works with iBuyers without seller representation, the seller has no protection or guidance. The iBuyers represent only their interests. Any legalities or rights the seller may have, the iBuyer is not obligated to let them know.

When iBuyers determine how much they will offer for your home (without ever viewing it) they know they can make a price adjustment after the inspection. After an offer is accepted, the iBuyer will conduct a full home inspection. That's the 2nd phase of price negotiation. The initial "price" can be reduced significantly once they determine how much it will cost them to repair/update to put it on the market to resell (at a profit of course.)

And finally an experienced advisor will guide you through the analysis of all the fees and ensure there are no hidden fees that ultimately takes a bite out of your hard earned equity.

So the bottom line is absolutely invite iBuyers to make an offer.They are buyers after all. Just be sure you are represented, protected, and well informed throughout the process.

Consider the situation for single mom Diane, who was struggling with the amount of time she had to spend driving to and from work. She could not buy a home closer to her work without first selling her current home. The challenge was the market conditions for her price range were extremely competitive -- multiple offers within the first few days of being listed. Sellers usually overlooked offers contingent on seller and existing home, in favor of non-contingent offers. She felt like her only option was to sell first then rent until she found a home to buy. That option filled her with dread – the double move, the double expense, the unknown timeframe for planning. Yet there was a solution. An iBuyer

In this case Diane would net more money by putting her home on the open market. However, the convenience factor of choosing her close date to lineup with her new home's closing meant she would avoid the energy and expense of a double move (moving to storage unit, then moving to new home plus storage fees, and time off work) and she would be able to make an offer that was more likely to be accepted by a seller.

A home just waiting to close that is already through the inspection and financing contingencies is far more appealing to a seller than one that is not yet on the market.

Here is a real life example of 2 investor offers and the fees they were charging the seller compared to current market value at the time.

| REAL LIFE SAMPLE: | Investor Offer #1 | Investor Offer #2 | Traditional MLS |
|---|---|---|---|
| Amount | $197,325 | $214,800 | $202,000 |
| Fee (%) | 7% | 5.5% | 6% |
| Service Fee | $13,813 | $11,814 | $12,120 |
| Other Fees (%) | — | 3% | — |
| Other Fees Amount | — | $6,444 | — |
| Repair Reduction | *Price based on current condition* | *Determined after contract* | *Price based on current condition* |
| Title Fees | $1,712 | $1,712 | $1,712 |
| **Totals** | **$181,800** | **$194,830** | **$188,168** |
| Repairs | — | -$10,000 | — |
| **Seller Net Total** | **$181,800** | **$184,830** | **$188,168** |

*NOTE: Initially, it seems offer #2 is the better option. However, after contract, the property was inspected and the buyer required a price reduction of $10,000 due to condition. The net seller was reduced to $184,830—less than traditional MLS.*

# Types of Buyers/ Financing and Why That's Important

## Cash

You have heard the saying "Cash is King". The cash buyer can purchase a home with no financing or mortgage. There is no underwriting and an appraisal is not required. However, many cash buyers do choose to get an appraisal to confirm market value. Cash buyers can purchase the home and all the contents if desired and close with very little red tape in a very short period of time. A cash buyer usually has a different mindset than a financed buyer. They often feel they are the driver and use their cash position to negotiate a lower price, especially if there are signs of seller distress. Cash can be the dangling carrot to a desperate seller. As tempting as it may be, if you follow the steps to prepare and properly market your home, you can sell to any buyer for fair market value.

## FHA Buyer

Launched in 1934 to help boost the housing market, the Federal Housing Administration (FHA) loan is still pretty much the same today. It's a government-backed loan that allows people to buy a moderately priced home with a down payment as low as 3.5 percent, with mortgage insurance required. This type of buyer is often a first-time home buyer just starting out, who may need seller assistance with closing costs. An FHA loan can sometimes signal weak financial position. FHA buyers can qualify with lower credit scores and may need gift assistance to cover their down payment and/or closing costs. Additionally the appraiser may require certain maintenance or repair items to be corrected as a condition of the buyer being approved for the loan. Another good reason to have your home inspected prior to marketing. No last minute costly surprises.

## VA Loan

VA loans are guaranteed by the United States Department of Veteran Affairs (VA). This is a great program for our veterans and military members currently serving in the US Military, reservists and surviving spouses that can be used to purchase single family homes, condos, manufactured homes and new construction. The intention is to supply home financing for eligible veterans to purchase with no money down. There are some down sides to accepting a VA loan. A strict home inspection and appraisal process often can make it impossible to buy a home "as is". If the seller won't agree to the repairs, either done in advance of settlement or putting money in an escrow account, a VA loan may not be approved. Also, there are fees which the VA prohibit from being charged to a VA buyer called "non-allowable fees". This is no reason to turn away this type of buyer.

## Conventional Loan

A conventional loan is a mortgage that is not guaranteed or insured by any government agency, including the Federal Housing Administration (FHA), the Farmers Home Administration (FMHA) and the Department of Veteran Affairs (VA). It is typically fixed in its terms and rate. Mortgages no guaranteed or insurance by these agencies are known as conventional loans and include Conforming loans, Non-conforming loans, Jumbo loans, Portfolio Loans and Sub-Prime Loans. About half of all conventional loans are called "conforming" mortgages, because they conform to guidelines established by Fannie Mae and Freddie Mac. These two government sponsored enterprises (GSEs) buy mortgages from lenders and sell them to investors. Their purpose is to make mortgages more widely available. This typical buyer will put down 10-20 percent down or more. There will be less restrictions on appraisals and inspections.

## 203K Loan

The Federal Housing Administration (FHA) administers the FHA 203(k) loan program, which makes it possible for buyers to purchase a property with the cost of repairs and improvements included in the loan. Since the program was designed to finance renovations and help revitalize neighborhoods, the required down payment may be as low as 3.5 percent of the total cost.

In addition to low down payments, the eligibility terms of an FHA 203(k) loan are more flexible. In general to be eligible for an FHA 203(k) loan, you must have a credit score of at least 620. Unlike other loans, you do not need to be a first-time home buyer in order to be eligible. If the renovation is extensive and you cannot live in the home during construction, up to six months of mortgage payments may be included in the FHA 203(k) loan, so you can avoid making double housing payments while living outside of the home.

Although some restrictions and special rules apply, 203(k) loans can be used to purchase and refurbish condos, two-to-four unit properties, and mixed-use properties, in addition to single-family residences and homes in planned unit developments. As a top 203(k) lender in the market, HomeBridge can lend you the maximum amount under a 203(k) loan, which is 96.5 percent of the after-improved value*. For refinancing, the maximum loan amount is 97.75 percent of the after-improved value.

## Private Financing

Sellers willing to take on the role of financier represent only a small fraction of all sellers -- typically less than 10%. That's because the deal is not without legal, financial, and logistical hurdles. But by taking the right precautions and getting professional help, sellers can reduce the inherent risks. These loans are often short term -- for example, amortized over 30 years but with a balloon payment due in five years. The theory is that, within a few years, the home will have gained enough in value or the buyers' financial situation will have improved enough that they can refinance with a traditional lender From the seller's standpoint, the short time period is also practical -- sellers can't count on having the same life expectancy as a mortgage lending institution, nor the patience to wait around for 30 years until the loan is paid off. In addition, sellers don't want to be exposed to the risks of extending credit longer than necessary.

# Conclusion

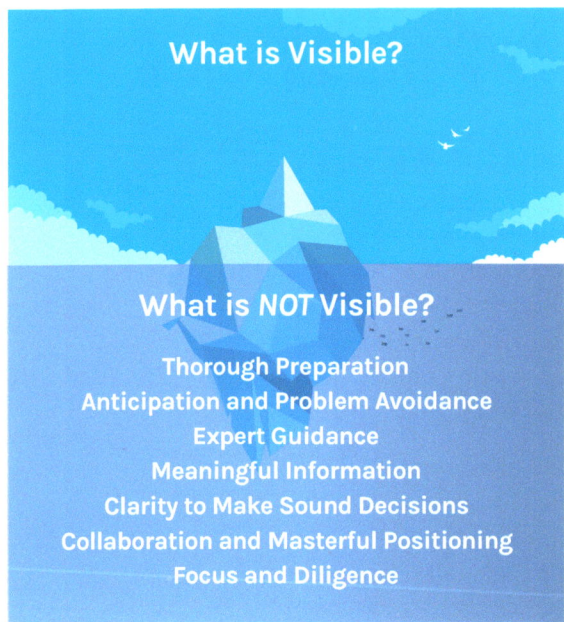

There is no shortage of technology advances that make things appear simple. Its tempting to assume what can be seen on the surface is all that needs to be considered. But, the fact is, real estate transactions are more complex and challenging than ever before.

Its worth reviewing the mindsets of successful sellers with a real life story of a cross country move for a special family.

When my sister and her husband made the decision to move from Illinois to Colorado, they faced the challenges I've helped hundreds of families navigate. It was fascinating to experience the whole process differently –one of supporter and confidante as opposed to the consultant, negotiator, and manager of all the integrated complexity.

They had a choice to make. Homes in their neighborhood were selling very quickly. So do they sell first and then look for a house in Colorado? That would mean a double move (with 2 kids, 2 dogs and a cat, 2 new jobs) They really did not want to rent or move twice. They were in a time crunch as they had new jobs to report to.

They learned from their very capable consultant that the market in Colorado was a seller's market and multiple offers were a common occurrence. A contingent offer would most likely be rejected by a seller in favor of a non-contingent offer.

Why? Think about things from a seller's perspective, we'll call them the Smiths. Lets say the Smiths have 2 offers. The Jones offer is $5000 but is NOT contingent them selling their home. The Parker's offer is $5000 higher but is contingent on their home closing. There are many risk factors to consider and yes, this is a common reason for 1 in 5 sales not closing.

# Contingencies

My sister had great advice from a local expert about the market conditions. They knew they would be facing multiple offers. Timing was critical so any offer they made would need to be as strong as possible. They had 2 challenges to overcome;

1. Competition from other buyers (there was low inventory and high buyer demand) and

2. Seller preference for non-contingent offers. This would have been the wrong time to try to negotiate a purchase price of less than market value.

It took 3 tries before my sister had an accepted offer. On the first try, a great property was available and did not yet have an offer acceptable to the seller – a very lucky situation in a seller's market. They made a strong offer – it was contingent on her home closing but her buyer's inspection period was already completed and was just waiting to close.

The close date meant they would avoid a double move. Great right? Well the sellers wanted to retain possession of the property for 3 days after close. "Post possession" is not uncommon. It is more common in a seller's market when buyers are competing for homes. There are potential risks that are unlikely, but if they occur, have consequences.

I've orchestrated many perfectly harmonious post and pre-possession agreements that cover risks for both sides. Knowing how to navigate those risks properly is critical.

In this case the sellers had a story in their mind that if they moved out the day before the actual close date, the buyers may not close and they would have completed their move. Now this is the standard practice and they didn't know anyone it had actually happened to, but someone told them it was a risk.

Regardless, the sellers had their story. My very stressed sister was struggling with the concept of post possession and created her story. What? I pay them for the house and I can't move in? So I have to pay to store our belongings, pay to stay at a hotel, pay for utilities, taxes, insurance, HOA fees because they are scared we won't close on time? That's completely unacceptable! These people don't want to sell. If they are this difficult now, it will be a nightmare during inspections and the rest of the process.! What if they don't move out on time? What if their movers damage something, what if there is a leak?

Now, this reaction is not at all typical for my sister. She manages extremely complex and intense projects with serious deadlines and major attitudes from multiple parties. However, she is human as we all are. She needed time to assess, to process, to weigh options, to get clarity on what was important to her family and what was not important.

The very last term - the last 10 feet to agreement was a compromise on the post possession. The sellers offered 1.5 days rather than 3 days. After some time to reflect and realize that what they had was far more I important than 1.5 days of post possession, my sister and her husband were able to move past the story they had created about the sellers. But they had not yet signed the counter agreeing to that compromise.

During that delay, the sellers received a cash offer (no contingency) for more money. Guess what? Sellers withdrew their counter offer and accept the higher non-contingent offer.

It was eye opening, even after helping so many folks, to witness the behind-the-scenes thinking that occurs during one of the most stressful events for most people - buying or selling a home. I knew there were private conversations

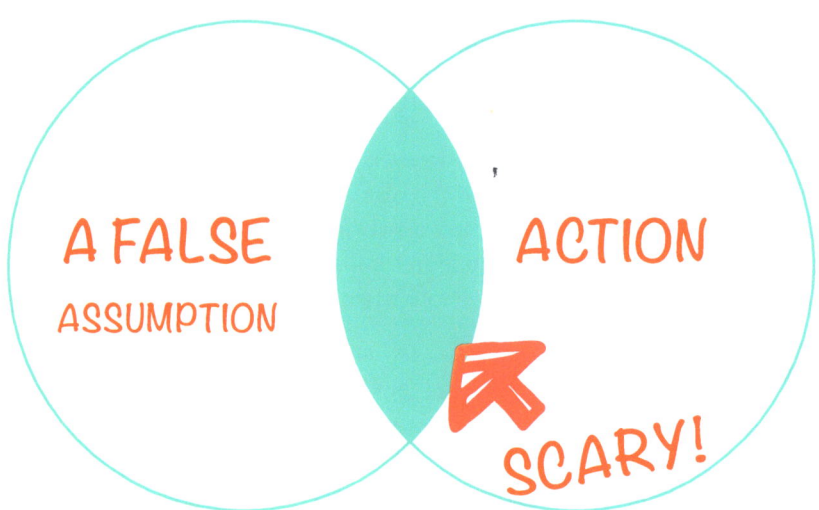

that influenced buyers and sellers. With my sister I had the unfiltered version of stories woven from fear, overwhelm and inaccurate assumptions.

In my sister's case, she had good mindsets #1 — **Ask Good Questions and Seek Meaningful Interpretation and #3 Seek Expert Advice.**

However, she struggled with mindset #2 — **Willingly Accept What Cannot be Changed, and Change What Can.** Once she moved to a higher mindset, the decision was clear. It was too late but it was clear!

That's why making decisions from the best possible mindset is so important. No one can know and plan for every situation ahead of time. Being aware of your mindset when making important decisions is something you can prepare for. And can guide you to make good informed decisions.moved to a higher mindset, the decision was clear. It was too late but it was clear!

# About the Author

**BETH REBENSTORF**

Beth Rebenstorf is the founder of the Rebe Homes Team, a top 1% producer in Arizona. Originally from the Chicago area she graduated from Arizona State University and spent 25 years as a sales and operations executive for computer and electronic payment services.

Since 2005 she has been leading, guiding, and protecting thousands of families throughout the Phoenix-Metro area as they move from where they are to where they want to be. Always with the intention of leaving each family better than how she found them.

When selling what is often the single largest asset for many families, diligent focus and expertise is needed each and every time. Beth believes navigating the
ever-changing real estate environment means providing not just information, but meaningful interpretation of the massive amounts of readily available information for various markets and specific situations. That's why 90% of her business is repeat clients and new clients introduced by those she has helped.

You can reach Beth at 480-236-8760, Beth@RebeHomes.com.

## Secrets You'll Discover

What to expect and how to best prepare you and your home for the home selling journey.

What the 10/10 rule of marketing is and why it's crucial to selling for the most money.

The best strategies for multiple offers.

How to make your home a box office hit.

How and Why the right Mindset makes a huge difference.

How Preparation and Marketing get buyers to pay more for your home.

The things that do and don't matter to market value.

Stories and insights of actual sellers and what they learned.

Top 10 Seller Mistakes

www.ingramcontent.com/pod-product-compliance
Lightning Source LLC
Chambersburg PA
CBHW040229220526
45473CB00001B/172